West Yorkshir

C000053264

on old picture po_____

Norman Ellis

1. Leeds Corporation tramcar No. 128 stands outside the Beckett's Arms at Meanwood terminus, awaiting departure for Leeds and Churwell. This tram had been a steam trailer car, but was electrified about 1901. It received a top cover in 1910 and lasted until 1927.

Designed and published by Reflections of a Bygone Age, Keyworth, Nottingham 2003

Printed by Adlard Print & Reprographics Ltd, Ruddington

£3.50

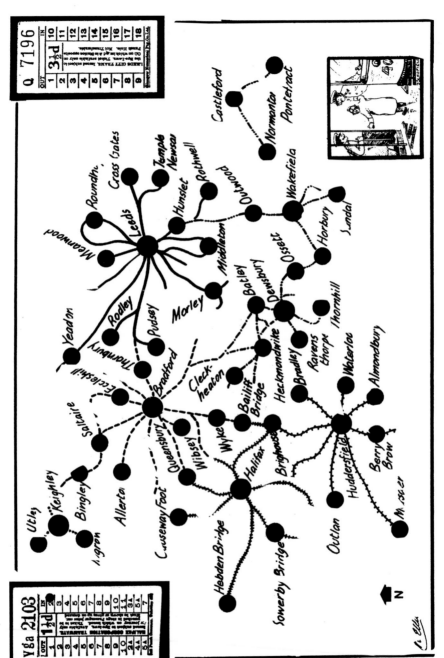

This simplified map of the West Yorkshire tramway network shows locations which feature in the book. Not all routes are included.

2. A charabanc and three Huddersfield Corporation tramcars feature on this view of Market Place and John William Street, Huddersfield. The tram on the left has a shorter balcony/canopy than the one on the right. The tram in the centre, dating from about 1912, has a more modern appearance and a protective screen for the driver, although the balcony is still open

Introduction

Formed in 1974, the Metropolitan County of West Yorkshire brought together a group of cities and towns whose development had been influenced by a variety of industries. Principal amongst these were coalmining and woollen manufacturing, although iron making, engineering, brickmaking, chemicals, pottery and brewing played an important part. The growth of the various factions had depended to some extent on their location, terrain and mineral reserves. Rivers and navigations, which provided a means for transportation, influenced their expansion. Most of the communities cherished the legacy of a historical past. For administrative purposes, the County of West Yorkshire is sub-divided into the Metropolitan Districts of Leeds, Bradford, Wakefield, Calderdale (including Halifax) and Kirklees (including Huddersfield and Dewsbury).

In the latter half of the nineteenth century, this largely industrialised section of the old West Riding attracted various railway companies who were eager to secure a share of the commercial business. Acquiring the passenger traffic was more of a problem. With many stations inconveniently sited, the passenger potential was not fully exploited. To a lot of people, the railways remained rather aloof. They eventually excelled at outings to the coast and country.

In the early 1900s, and for some time after, motor cars were a novelty rather than a neccessity. But the revolutionary electric trams entered the frame. They infiltrated the cities and towns and their suburbs. They delivered workers to the mills and mines. At weekends, families were able to have their pennyworth to the park. The tramcars were non-polluting, smooth-running and a decided improvement on the few horse buses, horse trams and steam trams, which plied the streets. Craftsmen-built and beautifully painted, they became the recognised mode of transport for the working class people, although even the well-to-do used them. Unfortunately, they fell victim to their own success. With a few alterations and routine maintenance, their lifespan often exceeded thirty years. By then, most of them looked dated.

This book covers five municipally-owned and three company-owned tramways. Four of them were built to the standard gauge of 4ft 8½in, but the remainder embraced four more different gauges. These factors inhibited the chance of developing a fully-integrated network, although running between Leeds and Bradford was made possible even though the gauges were different. At Ossett, where two tramways of the same gauge met, no regular through running materialised. The West Riding company's Castleford-based lines were never connected to the same company's Wakefield-based ones.

The municipalities were proud of their tramways. The companies, which had shareholders to consider, were frequently under attack from local councillors for not providing the best service. From the *Ossett Observer* of 8th December 1906: *"Alderman Ben Turner, secretary of the Dewsbury & District Trades & Labour Council, urged the council to press for reduced tram fares for children. Councillor Sykes expressed sympathy with the suggestion, and thought a better service of workmen's cars should also be asked for. The overcrowding at present was excessive. Councillor Myers said that the tramway system in the district was a bad system. It was irregular and there was no connection between the different routes. As to overcrowding, he mentioned a case in which the conductor said that he had 75 passengers aboard, and that was a danger to the public. There had been many complaints of children being charged full fare. Councillor Sykes said that a conductor told him that he had 91 passengers on the car. Councillor Cropper agreed that the workmen's cars were a disgrace to the tramway authorities. It was agreed to write to the manager of the tramways."*

continued on page 6

3. Leeds Corporation tramcar No. 136, new in 1899, enters Briggate from Boar Lane. Further up Briggate are another electric tram (No. 2), a horse tram and a steam tram, and in the distance some horse buses. This dates the photograph at 1901 at the latest, although the Photochrom card was posted in 1908.

4. A photograph taken about thirty years later from the same spot. Tram barriers have been erected in the centre of Briggate. Other types of transport are obviously on the increase. Commercial House, the new art-deco building on the left, accommodates the Fifty Shilling Tailors. An Excel series postcard.

Introduction
continued from page 4

What of the tramcars themselves in West Yorkshire? This was largely double-deck territory, although the Yorkshire Woollen fleet included sizeable batches of single-deckers. The earliest double-deck trams had open tops, which were open to the elements. Over a period, most of them received top covers. Later batches usually were supplied with covered upper decks. For many years, the seating norm was longitudinal inward-facing seats downstairs and reversible transverse seats upstairs. These later featured in many lower decks.

The three company-owned tramways were reluctant to modernise, although some West Riding cars were given higher-powered motors for the prestigious Wakefield to Leeds route. In the 1920s and 1930s, Huddersfield Corporation purchased several stylish modern cars. Leeds Corporation successfully pioneered the use of reserved track, its best known example being opened in 1925 to serve new housing estates at Middleton. With its progressive rolling-stock policy, it bought the aesthetically-pleasing 'Horsfields' in the 1930s. It tapped the secondhand market by purchasing batches of big ex-London 'Felthams'. The introduction of three single-deck railcars in 1953 should have augered well for the future. Instead, it seemed to presage the end. The last Leeds trams (and the last in West Yorkshire) ran in 1959.

Who used the trams? In West Yorkshire, some workers lived near their place of employment. Rows of houses rubbed shoulders with mills and factories. People were not daunted by having to walk a couple of miles to shop or visit friends. The Edwardians were, however, captivated by the trams. The fares were cheap when compared to those of earlier horse buses. But prudence was an issue, particularly with large families. The tram upper decks tended to be filled twice a day - morning and evening - with artisans and labourers. At other times, the ladies did venture upstairs. Children loved the open-ended balconies. Apart from the very rich and very poor, just about everybody used the trams at some time.

In 1906, Mr Silas Tuffley, secretary of the Lofthouse Colliery Company, who lived at the Laurels, Outwood, near Wakefield, boarded a tram at Thwaite Gate and paid the fare of 5d. He intended alighting at the Queen Hotel, Outwood, but due to a misunderstanding, was taken two hundred yards past. An argument ensued with the conductor. Tuffley decided to stay on the car, ride through to the depot at Belle Isle and protest to the manager. The conductor then asked Tuffley to pay the extra fare from Outwood to Belle Isle, but he refused. He was later summoned to appear at Wakefield West Riding Court and fined 2s 6d plus 31s 6d costs. A gentleman of some importance, Mr Tuffley was more used to issuing instructions than being told what to do.

The success of West Yorkshire's tramways was muted by a lack of corporate thinking. However, the tramcars did provide a convenient, frequent and reasonably-priced service. Long journeys and circular tours were possible by switching trams. But through-running between the different concerns was the exception rather that the rule. Today, the same area is covered by a number of bus companies, which operate partly under the aegis of Metro, whose motto is *"Here to get you there"*. Easier said than done on today's congested roads. It only needs a few men with shovels and temporary traffic lights to cause a complete foul-up. Enjoy the following photographs of the 'good old days'. All of them are taken from picture postcards in the author's collection.

Norman Ellis
July 2003

5. The photographer arrived early at Rodley to capture the inaugural car, No. 155, from Leeds on 6th July 1906, according to the caption (some doubt exists about the exact date). The tramcar, part of the 133-182 batch, was delivered from Brush of Loughborough in 1899. Card by the Phototype Co., Ventnor Street, Leeds.

6. *"The building is Benton Park Chapel just above the gasworks and the car will be a Yeadoner."* So wrote Annie on the back of this card, which depicts the opening of the extension from Horsforth to Yeadon on 26th May 1909. The tramcar was built by Leeds City Tramways in 1909. Another Phototype card.

7. *"Wishing you a plentiful harvest."* With this message, the card was posted from Hunslet Carr to Stowmarket, Suffolk, in 1905. Leeds tramcar No. 73, on Balm Road, Hunslet, awaits its return to the city. To the right are back-to-back properties on Taylor's Place, a fried fish and a chemist's shop. Phototype postcard.

8. Leeds tramcar No. 279 passes Harrison's Avenue on Stanningley Road at Swinnow. The car, purchased from Dick, Kerr of Preston in 1902, received its top cover in 1905. The evocative scene includes terraces, corner shops and two road sweepers. The card, by the Phototype Co., was posted from Stanningley to Pinchbeck, Lincolnshire, in 1907.

9. Looking smart in its chocolate, primrose and white livery, Leeds tramcar No. 320 is featured near Kirkstall Abbey in 1923. It was built at the Kirkstall Road works of Leeds City Transport in 1914, with seating for 22 in the lower saloon and 36 in the upper saloon, and 190⁰ reversed staircases. The driver is wearing gloves, even though the platform of the car has a protective screen. The conductor displays his ticket rack, bell-punch machine and cash bag. The knickerbockered boy may be waiting for a ride on the open balcony. And a famous Yorkshire newspaper gets a mention.

10. A splendid photograph in Church Lane, Pudsey. Trams reached Pudsey from Leeds in 1908, the line being an extension of an existing route to Stanningley. The tramcar, No. 282, was new in 1902, received a top cover in 1905 and was withdrawn in 1931. Note the 190^0 reversed stairway and huge fleet number.

11. Trams mingle with other forms of traffic on Boar Lane, Leeds, in the early 1940s. Nearest the camera is a 'Horsfield' car, new in 1931. Further along is a 'Chamberlain' car of 1926/7 vintage. They were named after general managers of Leeds City Tramways. Bamforth of Holmfirth postcard No. 154.

12. Parasol and baby doll. Plus an excellent view of Bradford Corporation tramcar No. 178, part of the 129-228 batch, delivered by G. F. Miles of Birkenhead in 1902-3. It seated 28 on the upper deck on transverse reversible seats and 22 in the lower saloon on longitudinal inward facing ones. Observe the driver's bell and direct half-turn stairs. The tram was withdrawn from service in 1919, although two further cars later carried the same fleet number.

13. Tramcar No. 7, of the first batch of sixteen electric cars introduced by Bradford Corporation in 1898, is pictured at Eccleshill terminus a few years later. One of the shops on the left incorporates a post office, whilst beyond it is the Mechanics' Institute.

14. Tram No. 67 was one of fifteen open-toppers supplied by Brush of Loughborough to Bradford Corporation in 1901. It is shown beside the Wesleyan Methodist Chapel at Allerton, c. 1905, after being fitted with a 'Bailey' top cover, so named after its designer, Albert Bailey, the Thornbury Depot foreman.

15. A tramway extension from Little Horton to Wibsey was inspected and opened on 9th October 1907. Bradford tramcar No. 25 is pictured taking part in the opening ceremony at the entrance to Wibsey's High Street. The car is bedecked with bunting, flags, plants - and civic dignitaries.

16. Bradford Corporation tramcar No. 190 was built as an open-topper by Milnes of Birkenhead in 1903. Within a couple of years, a 'Bailey' top cover had been fitted, as shown here. The car is featured at Wyke terminus, with the new board school (opened in September 1904) in the background.

17. A pair of Bradford cars, Nos. 204 and 247, await departure from tram barriers in Forster Square c. 1930, with the Midland (LMS) complex and YMCA in the background. At first glance, the tramcars look very similar, but there are subtle differences in the number and proportions of the windows.

18. Reorganisation after the 1914-18 War included the introduction of new Bradford trams and withdrawal or renumbering of older ones. Tramcar No. 222, the third to carry this number, arrived from makers English Electric, Preston, in 1921. It is pictured at Saltaire on a card by Matthews of Bradford, posted in 1923.

TRAM TERMINUS. WYKE.

19. Tramcar No. 193, the second to bear the number, was built by Bradford City Tramways in 1917. It stands resplendent at Wyke terminus, against an interesting background of buildings (board school on left) and tram standards, with the driver and conductor taking a rest. The Lilywhite card was posted from Wyke to Belfast in 1922.

20. This decorated and illuminated tram toured Bradford for the Coronation of King George V and Queen Mary in 1911. It is shown at the Thornbury Depot, which was started in 1900. The card, by Boocock Brothers, photographers, Barkerend, Bradford, was posted from the city to Halifax on 6th July 1911.

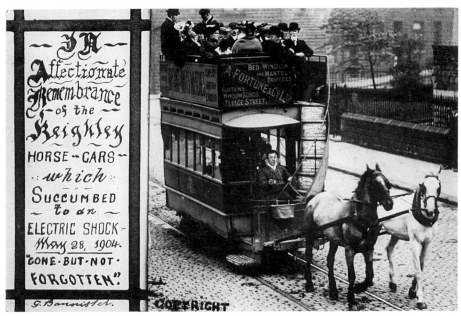

21. The Keighley Tramways Co. operated seven open-top double-deck horse trams between 1899 and 1904. An example of the four larger types, No. 2, is featured on this memorial card, issued in 1904.

22. Keighley Corporation reconstructed the original horse tram routes to take electric traction. Using electric tramcar No. 1, a successful trial run was made from the depot to Ingrow on 16th September 1904, where, as shown, an interested crowd gathered.

23. Following a Board of Trade inspection on the morning of 12th October 1904, the Keighley Corporation tramway was forthwith officially opened. In celebration, tramcars Nos. 2 and 3 were modestly decorated. Here, No. 2 is pictured at Utley, laden with civic dignitaries. The card was posted from Leeds to Headingley on 5th November 1904.

24. In 1910-12, Keighley's open-top cars were fitted with covers. Tram No. 5 is seen passing over Station Bridge. The card, by Jackson & Son, Grimsby and Bradford, was posted from Keighley to Brotton-in-Cleveland on 20th September 1919 with the message, *"Going to Bradford again today to see football match"*.

25. The conductor of Halifax Corporation tramcar No. 70 has problems with the trolley boom at King Cross, whilst a policeman looks on. The Prescott Fountain, an ornate tram standard, two elegant lamps and the adverts add atmosphere to this Edwardian scene. The card was produced by J.C. Swallow of Halifax.

26. The hilly terrain encountered by Halifax trams is epitomized by this view of Ovenden Road, to the north of Halifax. Tram No. 13 is pictured, being part of the second batch, delivered in 1898-99. Elderly men pass the time chatting in front of billboards.

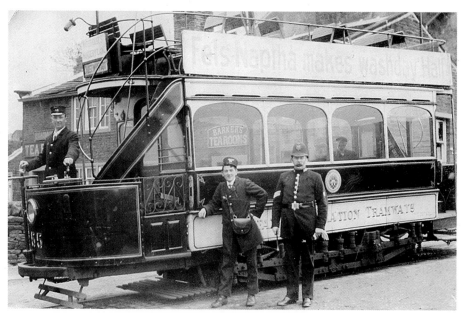

27. Tea rooms at Causeway Foot in Pennine moorland provide background for Halifax tramcar No. 55. Craftsmanship, paintwork (blue/white) and lining out look superb. The rocker panel shows the ownership; the waist panel the town coat of arms. The young man, Andrew Nash, conducted on Birmingham, Colne and Halifax tramcars, before becoming a Huddersfield tram driver.

28. Halifax tramcar No. 94, new in 1903, stands at Hebden Bridge terminus with another of the same batch (83-94). It has longer canopies for driver protection and curtains at the windows for passenger luxury. The moment was captured by Crossley Westerman of the Electric & Daylight Studio, West End, Hebden Bridge.

29. Halifax tramcar No. 65 was delivered from Brush of Loughborough with an open upper deck. It is shown after being fitted with a top cover by Halifax carpenter, Mr. C. Turner, in 1908. Because of the narrow gauge, the cover gives the car a rather gawky appearance. The direct type staircase looks steep and hazardous. A warning notice on the platform states that *"Passengers entering or leaving the car while in motion do so at their own risk"*.

UNION STREET. HALIFAX.

30. Although the Halifax fleet was mainly double-deck, a few single-deck cars were operated. Seen near the tram shelter, erected in 1912 on Union Street, Halifax, is clerestory-roofed tramcar No. 105. New in 1925, it seated 36 passengers. Lilywhite postcard No. HFX 432.

31. On 3rd August 1904, Halifax Corporation introduced a pair of one-man demi-cars. On 14th October 1904, one of them, No. 95, ran out of control down Horton Street, Halifax, and collided with its sister, No. 96. They were scarcely used after the crash. Here, No. 95 (plus another) is shown on Bradford Road, Brighouse, when new.

32. Open-top Halifax tramcar No. 88, new in 1903, was fitted with a top cover in 1912. Descending a setted Northgate, Halifax, a few years later, it has just passed Driver's - the famous Yorkshire grocers.

33. Early on the morning of 15th October 1907, Halifax tramcar No. 64 ran backwards out of control down the steep 1 in 9 Pye Nest Road in Sowerby Bridge. It left the rails at Bolton Brow, hit a wall and fell over. The conductor and ten passengers were killed; 37 passengers were injured. The postcard, one of several, shows the overturned tram and anxious onlookers.

34. Huddersfield Corporation was a steam tramway pioneer. Here, a steam engine (part hidden) and trailer emerge from Kirkgate, right. Two similar combinations traverse John William Street. Electric wires are up, and the last steam trams ran on 21st June 1902, so the view dates from before then, although postmarked 22nd September 1903.

35. The first batch of electric tramcars for Huddersfield Corporation, Nos. 1-25, was delivered from Milnes of Birkenhead in 1900. At Parkgate, Berry Brow, a shawled lady boards large bogie-car No. 16. Did she drop some postcards in the box on the dashboard? Huddersfield introduced these boxes (on steam trams) in 1893.

TRAM TERMINUS, ALMONDBURY.

36. New in 1902, Huddersfield tramcar No. 31 is seen at the Almondbury terminus, complete with its Tudor-arch windows - an embellishment not appreciated by upper floor passengers if they were wet and cold. This tram also carries a posting box.

TRAM TERMINUS WATERLOO

37. In weak winter sunshine, Huddersfield tramcar No. 34 stands at its terminus outside the Waterloo Hotel on Wakefield Road, c. 1905. New in 1902, the tram has plain side windows with ventilators above. Unusually, this car and a few more of the same batch, never received top covers. In later years, they were useful for moving Fartown's rugby supporters.

THE FIRST TRAM TO MARSDEN OCT 3 1914   O. WARD PHOTO

38. Although electric trams reached Slaithwaite in 1901, the extension to Marsden was not opened until 3rd October 1914. The inaugural tramcar, No. 95, is pictured in Marsden, being one of ten purchased in 1913, with folding platform doors but 'fresh air' balconies.

39. Because of the 1914-18 War, introduction of a tram service from Huddersfield to Brighouse, via Rastrick, was deferred until 12th March 1923. Decorated inaugural car, Huddersfield No. 78, is depicted after arrival at Brighouse terminus in Bradford Road at midday. Public service commenced in the afternoon.

40. At the terminus in Outlane, the highest point on the Huddersfield tramway system, car No. 70 stands against a background of old buildings and distant hills. This 1903 tram received a top cover in 1905, and is shown shortly after, complete with posting box. Card produced by S. Carter, Netherton.

41. On the morning of Saturday 22nd April 1905, Huddersfield tramcar No. 24 ran out of control down the hill at Bradley and ended in a copse. There were no fatalities. The postcard admirably shows the design of the large bogie car, new in 1900, and supplied with a top cover in 1903.

42. Northgate, at the edge of Dewsbury's Market Place, served as the town's tramway centre. It is shown in the late 1920s, with Yorkshire (Woollen District) tramcar No. 69, a 36-seater, new from Brush in 1905, and awaiting departure to Ravensthorpe. Single-deckers were used on this route because of low bridges.

43. Clerestory-roofed YWD tramcars Nos. 57 and 58 were delivered from Brush in 1903. They were similar to the 1 to 6 batch bought in 1902. All of them were used on the Ravensthorpe route. Car No. 58 looks resplendent at Ravensthorpe terminus. Note the driver's bell, used to warn jaywalkers and straying dogs.

44. YWD tram No. 15, one of the 7-48 batch of open toppers delivered in 1902-3, negotiates a narrow part of Town Street, Cleckheaton. Within a year, these cars started to acquire top covers. The card, by well-known local photographer J. Hodgson of Cleckheaton, was posted from there to nearby Littletown on 9th December 1905.

45. Yorkshire Woollen tramcar No. 11, glimpsed in Heckmondwike Market Place, commenced life in 1902 with an open upper deck. Having undergone several overhauls, it appears here in its post-war and final form, with high and solid curved panels on the balconies. Doncaster Rotophoto card No. 413-4.

46. Two YWD tramcars stand at Thornhill terminus, near the entrance to Combs Pit, two miles south of Dewsbury, in 1905. The open-topped one is No. 18. The other is part of the same batch, but has been given a top cover. The Whitsuntide procession is in progress.

47. Floods in Batley and Dewsbury were a periodic nightmare. This washout in Batley Carr on 25th May 1925 shows, left to right: YWD car No. 8; a YWD single-decker of the 70-81 batch; Batley Corporation car No. 51. Batley Corporation tramcars were leased to the Yorkshire Woollen company.

48. Two tram inspectors posture in front of an unidentified tramcar of the Dewsbury, Ossett & Soothill Nether Tramways, outside the depot in Church Street, Ossett. The car must be part of the batch purchased from Brush in 1908, numbered 1 to 8, and seating 22 in the downstairs saloon and 32 above. The direct type stairway is visible, although the livery of dark red and broken white has to be imagined. The postcard was produced by Mark Cross of Borough Studio, 40 Market Place, Dewsbury.

49. A D&O tramcar of the 1 to 8 batch travels up Ossett's Dale Street on the last lap of its journey from Dewsbury. The old Ossett Co-operative Society buildings are on the left. The card was posted from Ossett to Sutton-in-Ashfield in 1915. Between then and 1925, the trams received top covers.

50. On 12th October 1915, D&O tramcar No. 3, the 4.15pm from Earlsheaton, ran out of control after entering the Wakefield Road cutting. It gained speed, overran the terminus near Dewsbury Town Hall and embedded itself in Hilton's shoe shop, as portrayed on this card from Mark Cross of Dewsbury.

51. The principal depot for Yorkshire (West Riding) tramcars was built on the site of a former dyeworks at Belle Isle, to the south of Wakefield. The generating station, seen here under construction on 28th April 1904, was adjacent to the sheds. This card, and several which follow, was produced by Edwin I. Walker, photographer, 28 Wood Street, Wakefield.

52. Workmen have stepped aside to provide an unhindered view of tracklaying in Westgate, Wakefield, in 1904. Track is being positioned on a bed of concrete, mixed on a wooden platform shown in the centre. Granite setts, piled at the roadside, await laying between and on each side of the rails.

53. Cable is being laid on Leeds Road, between Lofthouse Gate and Outwood (in the distance). Side poles with bracket arms are in position, but not track. Various substations were fed from the main generators at Belle Isle via cables. Those shown here ran to the substation at Rothwell Haigh. Card by E.I. Walker, Wakefield.

54. West Riding tramcar No. 13 enters the Bull Ring, Wakefield, on the first test run on 22nd July 1904. The destination blind shows Castleford, but this town was never connected to Wakefield by tram. Another postcard by E.I. Walker.

55. The West Riding system was opened to the public on 15th August 1904. Thirty trams were delivered from the Electric Railway & Tramway Carriage Works at Preston. One of them (No. 10, 20 or 30) is featured in the depot yard at Belle Isle. Note the curtains and reversed stairs. The card is postmaked 25th August 1904.

56. WR tramcar No. 73 climbs Upper Kirkgate, Wakefield, on its way to Horbury and Ossett. This is one of eight trams hired in 1917 from Leeds Corporation, to replace ones lost in a fire at Castleford Depot. They were sold to the WR in 1919. Valentine of Dundee postcard 91966 JV.

57. WR tram No. 42 descends Benton Hill, Horbury, bound for Wakefield and Agbrigg, c. 1912. It was part of the second batch, Nos. 31-55, delivered from the Preston works in 1905, complete with top covers, and seating 22 passengers in the lower saloon and 34 above. Card by Herbert Myers Wilson, Wood Street, Wakefield (successor to Walker).

58. A boy carries morning papers, a cart delivers milk, and West Riding tramcar No. 35 starts its inaugural run from Castleford to Pontefract on a damp Monday morning, 29th October 1906, the date when Normanton, Castleford and Pontefract trams began carrying paying passengers.

MARKET PLACE, NORMANTON.

59. Standing at its terminus in the Market Place, Normanton, West Riding tramcar No. 30 is about to depart for Pontefract, via Castleford. The car had been delivered to Wakefield in 1904, was transferred to the Castleford section in 1906, but returned to Wakefield in 1927.

E.L.S. 39-1. MARKET STREET, PONTEFRACT.

60. WR tramcar No. 37 is featured at the Pontefract terminus in Market Street. New to Wakefield in 1905, the car was moved to Castleford Depot in 1906, and destroyed during the fire there in 1917, along with others. A new tram numbered 37 was purchased in 1920. E.L. Scrivens card No. 39-1.